THEN & NOW

MACON

Opposite: A mule-drawn wagon leisurely makes its way up Mulberry Street in the late 1800s. (Courtesy Middle Georgia Archives, Washington Memorial Library, Macon.)

MACON

Glenda Barnes Bozeman

This book is dedicated to my daughter, Summer Brittany Bozeman, my own personal cheerleader, who blazed the trail, cleared the path, lit the way, held my hand, and walked with me on this journey. Her courage and willingness to take risks amazes and inspires me. Without her, this project would never have been conceived or completed. And to my husband, Jim Bozeman, who endured late meals, or missed them altogether, when I lost myself in the work.

Library of Congress Control Number: 2009934795

Published by Arcadia Publishing
Charleston, South Carolina

Printed in the United States of America

Then and Now is a registered trademark and is used under license from
Salamander Books Limited

For all general information contact Arcadia Publishing at:
Telephone 843-853-2070
Fax 843-853-0044
E-mail sales@arcadiapublishing.com
For customer service and orders:
Toll-Free 1-888-313-2665

Visit us on the Internet at www.arcadiapublishing.com

ON THE FRONT COVER: The Macon armory was home to a volunteer militia group that fought in every American war up to World War II and the site of many glittering balls and social events. (Then image courtesy Middle Georgia Archives, Washington Memorial Library, Macon; now image courtesy of the author.)

ON THE BACK COVER: Macon's Confederate monument is in its original location in front of the Bibb County Courthouse in this 1886 image of Mulberry and Second Streets. (Courtesy Middle Georgia Archives, Washington Memorial Library, Macon.)

CONTENTS

ACKNOWLEDGMENTS

For their assistance in researching and compiling this information, and for much appreciated advice, I would like to acknowledge and thank the following individuals: Jack and Katherine Thomas, Dan Morton, Carolyn Kennedy (Mulberry Street United Methodist Church), Jo McConnell and Sadie Crumbley (*Macon's Treasures Remembered*), Bob Rush (St. Paul's Episcopal Church), Josh Rogers and Vicki Hertwig (Historic Macon Foundation), Melanie Vaughn, Dr. Milton Johnson, Summer Bozeman, Linda Doll, Anne Rogers, Sandy Goolsby, Muriel Jackson, Steve Engerrand, Gail DeLoach, Christopher Stokes, Willard Rocker, Vicki Akin, Kim Zwally-Kepfer, Sue and Ron Bloodworth, and Marilyn Madden and Bill Hodges, whose friendship supports me in all my endeavors.

Unless otherwise noted, all vintage images are courtesy of the Middle Georgia Archives at Washington Memorial Library in Macon, Georgia, and all modern photographs are the work of the author.

INTRODUCTION

The site on the Ocmulgee River that was to become Macon has been inhabited for at least 10,000 years. Ancient American Indian mounds preserved at the Ocmulgee National Monument in east Macon give testament to the civilizations that once settled on the banks of the Ocmulgee River. The city of Macon's earliest beginnings were at Fort Hawkins overlooking the Ocmulgee mounds, across the river from the Macon of today.

In 1806, Revolutionary War hero Benjamin Hawkins was sent by Pres. Thomas Jefferson to build a fort on the east side of the Ocmulgee River, the western frontier of Georgia at the time. He was also under orders to negotiate peace with the Creek Indians and to monitor American Indian activity within the state. The fort attracted trappers, traders, and the families of soldiers garrisoned there. Wagons continually arrived with newcomers, especially from North Carolina. A community dubbed Newtown grew up around the fort.

A treaty with the Creek Indians in 1821 made the land on the west side of the river available for settlement, and some of Newtown's population moved across the river, where they were joined by settlers from other British colonies. It was there that Macon was established in 1823. Newtown became a part of Macon, and a bridge was constructed to connect the settlements on both sides of the river.

Unlike some frontier towns that occurred haphazardly, the founders of Macon, inspired by the city of Babylon, laid plans with wide avenues, flowering medians, and parks interspersed throughout the city. It was their intention to create a city within a park. A city ordinance was instituted requiring homeowners to plant trees in front of their homes, and these early plans are responsible for the tree-lined streets and blooming parks of today. Even the cemeteries were parks, with waterfalls, ponds, and paths for strolling—virtual gardens of graves.

Steamboats began docking in Macon in 1829, and stagecoaches traveled regularly between Macon and Milledgeville, the state capital at the time. Railroads came to Macon in 1833, bringing expanded commerce and residents to an already booming metropolis. In that year, a South Carolina senator applauded Macon as "the queen inland city of the South."

Macon enjoyed such phenomenal success due to its location on the Ocmulgee River, its position as the hub of 11 rail lines, its central location in the state, its proximity to the fruit-producing orchards and cotton-growing fields of Georgia, and the availability of natural resources such as kaolin and clay used in various manufacturing processes and brick making. Fortunes were made almost overnight, and Macon reflected the affluence of its early citizens, who built gracious mansions and handsome public buildings.

Cotton remained the mainstay of the area's economy, and Macon joined with other Georgia cities and seceded from the Union in 1861. Due in large part to its central location and position as the hub of the state's railroad lines, wounded soldiers, displaced families, and refugees poured into Macon during the Civil War. Buildings were converted from other uses to be utilized as hospitals, and concerned citizens built orphanages to house children left parentless by the war.

A large portion of Georgia met with destruction during the war, including nearby Clinton and Griswoldville, which were decimated. But because of Sherman's mistaken impression of a massing of Confederate troops at Macon, the city escaped damage. As Sherman approached, Gov. Joseph Brown, who had come to Macon fleeing Union advances into Milledgeville, issued a desperate call to arms via the *Macon Telegraph* on July 30, 1864, stating, "The enemy is now within sight of your houses. We lack force. I appeal to every man, Citizen or Refugee, who has a gun of any kind, or can get one, to report to the Courthouse with the least possible delay, that you may be thrown in to the companies and aid in the defense of the city. A prompt response is expected from every patriot."

Macon responded, and by 7:00 p.m. that same day, 2,000 men gathered, prepared to defend their city, including the Silver Grays, a full company of aged gentlemen. Men who were conveniently passing through Macon at the time—600 Tennesseeans from Andersonville and 1,000 state troops on their way to Atlanta—were temporarily detained. Sherman bypassed Macon and continued on his ruinous path through Georgia.

Macon struggled during the Reconstruction period along with the rest of the South, but unlike other cities faced with rebuilding, Macon rapidly regained its footing. Continuing growth in the 1900s and expansion of the city's commercial interests from cotton production and other types of agriculture to include tin products, furniture, coaches, carriages, leather wares, and iron and brass manufacturing, ensured Macon's prosperity into the first half of the 20th century.

Academic and cultural pursuits thrived during the prewar days as they would after the Civil War. Wesleyan College was established in 1836 and was the world's first institution chartered to issue diplomas to women. In 1871, Mercer University moved to Macon from its original location in Penland, Georgia, and expanded its purview from a young men's seminary to a coed university with 11 major fields of study. Private schools and academies were established for the education of the city's youth, and private education is still a strong Macon tradition today. Elam Alexander, a prominent Macon architect and builder concerned about education for the city's poor children, left instructions in his will that a trust be established to build public schools. Two Alexander schools established under these provisions continue to operate into the present.

The 1950s and 1960s saw a new era of music and culture emerging and evolving in Macon that would soon reach the rest of the nation and influence the entire world of music. In the early 1950s, "Little Richard" Penniman was washing dishes at the Macon Greyhound bus station cafeteria by day and singing at Anne's Tic Toc Room by night. In 1955, soul singer James Brown recorded his first single, "Please, Please, Please," at WIBB Studios on Mulberry Street. In 1960, Otis Redding, who grew up singing in the choir of Vineville Baptist Church, made his debut at the Douglass Theatre.

The Allman Brothers Band, known as the architects of Southern rock, moved to Macon in 1969 in order to record with legend Phil Walden's Capricorn Records. Their sound—fusing blues, rock, jazz, rhythm and blues, and country—created a new genre which would define music and culture for the next decade and beyond. Macon became the home of Southern rock, the soul of the South, producing other greats such as Wet Willie and the Marshall Tucker Band.

Macon is the cherry blossom capital of the world with 250,000 cherry trees, more than 10 times the number of Washington, D.C. It is known for beauty and is a favorite stop on Georgia's Antebellum Trail. One of the great historic cities of the American South, Macon has earned its distinction as the heart and soul of Georgia.

CHAPTER 1

DOWNTOWN STREET SCENES

Many of the buildings in Macon's historic downtown are from the 19th and early 20th centuries. Historic buildings, tree-lined streets, and blooming parks give downtown a distinct Old South personality and appearance. This 1908 photograph was taken from the top of the Grand Opera House looking toward Walnut Street and the river.

11

The Mulberry and Second Street intersection has been anchored by the Washington Block building since 1857, when it was constructed on the site of Washington Hall, one of Macon's earliest stagecoach stops and hotels, which burned in 1855. The Masonic lodge building seen in this 1879 photograph has since replaced by the tall American Federal building, as seen in the current photograph. Also absent from the modern photograph is the militia headquarters building, whose site is now a parking lot.

DOWNTOWN STREET SCENES

This 1894 photograph was taken 15 years after the previous image on the same block of Mulberry Street but from the opposite end of the block. A gentleman reads his newspaper (far left) in the door of a café in the space that has continuously housed a restaurant since 1892. A youngster sits on the curb in front of the Masonic hall, which has been replaced by the high-rise building in the photograph below. The militia headquarters building site is now a vacant lot.

The Confederate monument is in its original position in front of the Bibb County Courthouse in this 1886 view of Mulberry and Second Streets. On the left is the Hardeman Building prior to its Victorian renovation. The steeple of First Presbyterian Church can be seen behind it.

The steeple at the center of the image, that of Mulberry United Methodist Church, was replaced by the castle-like turrets of the current structure after the previous building burned. Trees in the median now obscure the buildings on the left.

In the center of the 1894 view of Mulberry Street looking north from Third Street below is the monument to William Wadley, president of the Central of Georgia Railway from 1866 to 1882. Wadley is remembered for taking a railroad that had seen hundreds of miles of track destroyed by war and restoring rail service and prosperity to Macon.

In the 1908 view below of Mulberry Street looking north from Third Street, a streetcar is about to pass in front of the Hotel Lanier. The clock tower of the Bibb County Courthouse and the Grand Opera House with its newly constructed office building facade can be seen in the distance. A parking garage and high-rise building now occupy the Hotel Lanier site, and the brick courthouse building was replaced by the current structure in 1924.

At the center of this 1908 photograph of the angle formed by Cotton Avenue and Second Street is the Hart Building, initially the Commercial and Savings Bank. The building has seen many uses but still retains its marble floors, brass teller cages, and stately bank appearance. The Confederate monument shown in front of the Hart Building in the current photograph below was moved from its original location in front of the courthouse in 1956.

The cornerstone of Macon's Confederate monument was laid in 1878 by the Ladies' Memorial Association. In this 1878 photograph, the monument's base is shown with a temporary column and Grecian urn prior to the completion and installation of the Confederate soldier sculpture. The monument's official dedication took place in 1879 with the 10-foot-tall Confederate soldier in position. The building in the background is the Hardeman Building prior to its Victorian renovation.

The Confederate monument at its original location in front of the courthouse, out of the photograph at right, appears to be floating above the streetcar at the intersection of Mulberry and Second Streets in the 1890 view below. At the center of the image is the Hardeman Building, seen with its undulating facade of bay windows, added when the building was remodeled in the late 1890s, in contrast to its original appearance in the photograph on the previous page.

This 1885 scene on Cotton Avenue shows a mule-drawn streetcar, Macon's first public transportation, in front of Hardeman Building and the Burke Printing and Publishing Company. Burke Publishing was an important institution in Macon beginning in the reconstruction era and grew to become one of Georgia's leading printers. The business closed in 1959 after nearly 100 years in operation. The Hardeman Building was remodeled in the 1890s to its current Victorian appearance.

The north side of Cotton Avenue, seen looking east in this 1894 image, shows the business of John C. Holmes and Company wholesale and retail grocers at the northeast corner of Cherry Street and Cotton Avenue. Rader and Company Jewelers now occupies the Holmes Grocery site, and the Big "O" (Otis Redding) Foundation, Bibb Music, Golden Bough Bookstore, and other retail establishments occupy this block of Cotton Avenue today.

Across the street from the former image, this 1908 photograph shows the Citizen's National Bank on the southeast corner of Cherry Street and Cotton Avenue. At the right side of the image is the rounded brick facade of the Roy G. Williams Pharmacy, which became a popular hangout for Macon teens in the 1950s and 1960s. The building is obscured by trees in the modern photograph but is still a popular gathering place as the Greek Corner Deli.

The 1908 photograph below shows the northwest corner of Third and Cherry Streets, the heart of Macon's business district at the time. The Fourth National Bank, one of the largest financial institutions in Georgia, was located on the site formerly occupied by Ralston Hall, a theatrical house that had burned 50 years before, in the building originally constructed for the Exchange Bank in 1891. Fourth National Bank failed in November 1928 after a two-hour run on the bank depleted its cash, creating one of the largest bank failures in the history of American banking and precipitating a run on all Macon banks.

The west side of Cherry Street, seen in the 1894 view below, shows Cherry further north than the previous photograph. The building with the eagle on top at the center of the historical photograph is home to the *Telegraph and Messenger*, forerunner to Macon's current newspaper, *the Macon Telegraph*.

The 5-foot-tall gilded eagle moved from location to location as the business moved and now is on display in the lobby of their current offices on Broadway. Willingham Furniture, the ornate building with onion-topped turrets, can be seen across Second Street.

Bales of cotton, ready for shipping, are stacked in the middle of Second Street between Poplar and Cherry Streets outside of the Willingham cotton warehouse in 1909. The ornate building next to the cotton warehouse at the corner of Cherry and Second Streets is Willingham Furniture, seen in the previous photograph from a different angle. The only structure readily identifiable in both photographs is the curved brick turret of the Willingham building, on the right of both pictures.

The south side of Second Street, farther east toward Mulberry Street than the previous photograph, shows shoppers on foot and in carriages in 1907. McKay Tailors, the T. A. Coleman Book Company, Commercial Printing, and Macon Phonograph were businesses at this location at the time. Across the street in the Hardeman Building on the left were the W. L. Williams Art Store and the Idle Hours Florist. Beyond the Hardeman Building is the clock tower of the Bibb County Courthouse.

The American National Bank on the southeast corner of Third and Cherry Streets, seen below in 1908, was diagonally across the street from the Fourth National Bank. Bank of America occupies the site today, keeping the banking tradition at that location alive. Keeping other downtown traditions alive, NewTown Macon is a nonprofit organization that encourages downtown revitalization and renovation. It is located next-door to Bank of America on Cherry Street, in the building with the arched door.

The median of Poplar Street on market day was crowded with the wagons of farmers who gathered to sell their products prior to the construction of the City Market building there in 1888. The City Market site is now Proudfit Park, named for an advocate of the City Market, and is fittingly utilized each Saturday by the City Market on the Green.

The City Market building, located in the median of Poplar Street from 1888 to 1916, is seen in the background of this 1905 photograph of mule-drawn wagons. The prominent building with the arched windows near the center of the photograph is the Southern Bell Telephone Exchange. The building was constructed on the corner of Poplar and Second Streets in 1904, after Temple Beth Israel demolished their original structure in 1902 and rebuilt at a different location because of the noise of the market.

DOWNTOWN STREET SCENES

The main point of entry to Macon from the east was this wooden covered bridge over the Ocmulgee River, shown in 1876. Originally constructed in 1826 to connect Newtown and Macon, it was built and rebuilt many times before being replaced with a steel structure. It stands today as the Otis Redding Bridge, named for Macon's famous native son. It is visible in the background of Gateway Park, below, which is the beginning of Macon's river walk, called the Ocmulgee Heritage Trail.

CHAPTER 2

PUBLIC BUILDINGS, HOTELS, AND ORGANIZATIONS

The lady in the fountain caused quite a stir (or more appropriately, waves) when she was placed in front of the county courthouse in 1913 by then-mayor Bridges Smith. It is evident in the photograph that she had male admirers, but the ladies of Macon strenuously objected to her nudity. The controversy attracted national attention, and she was removed in 1918 by Smith's successor, Glen Toole.

The Bibb County Courthouse was built in 1870 at a cost of $130,000. Its clock tower contained Macon's second town clock, the first having been removed from the previous courthouse and installed in the steeple of First Presbyterian Church across Mulberry Street. The clocks rarely agreed on the time, creating a cacophony of chimes and confusion, which prompted the removal of the church's steeple clock to end the noisy competition. The Victorian courthouse building was replaced in 1924 by the brick and marble building at the same location. (Courtesy Georgia Archives Vanishing Georgia Collection BIB-88.)

PUBLIC BUILDINGS, HOTELS, AND ORGANIZATIONS

Macon City Hall was built in 1837 as headquarters for the Monroe Railroad and Banking Company and later was utilized as a fireproof cotton warehouse before serving as city hall beginning in 1860. During the Civil War, it was used as a military hospital. Its greatest distinction came on November 18, 1864, when it served as the Georgia state capitol. Gov. Joseph Brown, fleeing the Union army's advances into Milledgeville (Georgia's capital at the time), moved the capital to Macon and set up in city hall. The last meeting of the Georgia Legislature under the Confederacy was held there. The building ceased to serve as the capitol in March 1865.

The Post Office and Federal Building was built in 1889 on the corner of Third and Mulberry Streets with the post office at street level and the federal courthouse and offices on upper floors. The structure seen in the current photograph replaced the earlier brick structure in 1908, and the post office and federal courthouse again shared the building. In 1963, a new post office was built on College Street at the original site of Wesleyan College, which had moved to Forsyth Road. The post office relocated to the new building, leaving the 1908 structure for exclusive use as the federal building.

PUBLIC BUILDINGS, HOTELS, AND ORGANIZATIONS

Macon's first official city auditorium was a wooden building hastily constructed in 1917 for a massive music festival, the Chautauqua of the South. It was razed in 1924 to make way for the current auditorium, a Greek Revival structure built of limestone and topped by one of the largest copper domes in the world. The former YMCA building can be seen on the right across Cherry Street in the current photograph.

The Academy of Music, built in 1884 with the largest stage in the Southeast and renamed the Grand Opera House in the 1960s, saw extravagant productions, including *Ben Hur* with live horses running on treadmills, and Harry Houdini, who left his legacy of trapdoors in the stage floor. The office building facade was added to the front of the academy building in 1905, but the elaborate auditorium was left intact. By the 1920s, the building was in decline and used almost exclusively for movies. By the 1960s, it had ceased showing movies, and plans were made to replace it with a parking lot. The Macon Arts Council saved it in 1967 and began restoration. Today it is managed by Mercer University as a live theater.

Completed in 1885 and restored in 2005, the armory building was the home of the Macon Volunteers, a militia unit founded in 1825 that doubled as a civic organization and social club. The volunteers, who fought in every war up to World War II, when they were absorbed into the Georgia National Guard, answered Texas's call for freedom from Mexico in 1836. They carried with them a flag of white silk with a centered blue star made by Joanna Troutman of Bibb County. This flag flew over the convention of Texas delegates who met to declare the independence of the Texas Republic and was adopted as the official flag of the Republic of Texas.

In the 1800s, militia units, fire brigades, and other fraternal organizations served important social functions. Macon's Masonic lodge, organized in 1824, has been described as the first society in the town of Macon. In 1846, the Grand Lodge of Georgia moved from Milledgeville to this building on Mulberry Street, shown in the 1876 photograph by C. Seaver Jr. The Masonic building's site is now occupied by the American Federal Building. (Courtesy of Georgia Archives Vanishing Georgia Collection BIB-73.)

PUBLIC BUILDINGS, HOTELS, AND ORGANIZATIONS

Before construction of Terminal Station, Georgia's grandest surviving railroad station, each rail line had its own passenger depot. In 1854, a compromise was worked out between the highly competitive railroads that allowed their individual lines to connect, clearing the way for a consolidated terminal, and in 1916, Terminal Station was built at the foot of Cherry Street at a cost of $1 million. Terminal Station once handled 100 trains per day but was closed in 1975 due to the decline in rail travel. The building was purchased by the City of Macon in 2002 and is being renovated to accommodate event space. (Courtesy of Georgia Archives Vanishing Georgia Collection BIB 247-82.)

This turreted building was erected in 1889 on Mulberry Street for the public library and historical society, which together occupied the second floor. The ground level was leased to commercial enterprises and initially housed a coffin shop. In the 1920s, the library moved to Washington Avenue, where a larger building was constructed as the result of a gift by Ellen Washington Bellemy of a lot and $50,000 for a building as a memorial to her brother, Hugh Washington. The church building on the right is First Presbyterian Church.

As the railroad hub of Georgia, Macon was flooded with casualties during the Civil War. Temporary hospitals were set up but ceased to exist after the war as the organizations housing them went back to normal operations. Macon had no hospital until 1894, when the need for a facility to care for the city's ill and injured poor was recognized. The Macon Hospital Association was formed, and it purchased the James Calloway mansion at 820 Pine Street, the center building in this photograph, where it opened Macon Hospital, originally consisting of 4 private and 16 ward beds. Expansions in 1898 and 1901 were just the beginning of its growth—Macon Hospital became the Medical Center of Central Georgia and is Georgia's second largest hospital today. (Courtesy of the Medical Center of Central Georgia.)

Built in 1910 at Cherry and First Streets, this grand building was erected at a cost of $75,000. A private men's club for a short while before being purchased by the YMCA, who occupied the building until the mid-1960s, it provided every convenience. In addition to sleeping rooms, it included reception halls, parlors, reading rooms, an auditorium, a gymnasium, marble showers, a swimming pool with constantly running spring water, bowling alleys, and a running track. It is now the Macon Health Club.

PUBLIC BUILDINGS, HOTELS, AND ORGANIZATIONS

The City Market, built in 1888 in the median of Poplar Street at First Streets is seen in the 1905 photograph below. The building was razed in 1916 and was replaced by Proudfit Park, named for Alexander Proudfit, who had advocated the building of the market. The monument to Southern women, placed by their husbands, fathers, and children, stands in Proudfit Park near the City Market location to honor the sacrifices of Southern women during the Civil War.

Rose Hill Cemetery, built in 1840 overlooking the Ocmulgee River and called a garden of graves, is an outstanding example of 19th century rural cemetery parks reminiscent of the terraced gardens of northern Italy. Rose Hill was designed by Simri Rose, who was instrumental in establishing the parks that still grace Macon's downtown. Rose Hill is the burial site for many of Macon's notable citizens, historic and recent, including two Allman Brothers Band members and "Little Martha," whose grave maker inspired an Allman Brothers song.

The Lanier House, built in 1850 and shown in this 1905 photograph, was considered one of the best and most comfortable Southern hotels and was owned by the grandparents of Georgia poet Sidney Lanier. Georgia governor Joseph Brown made his home there during the Civil War, when the state capital was moved from Milledgeville to Macon to escape Sherman's onslaught. After Jefferson Davis and his family were taken into custody in Irwinton, they were brought to the Lanier, where the Federals occupying Macon maintained their headquarters. The Lanier Hotel was demolished in 1975, and a high-rise building and parking garage were constructed on the site.

The Brown House, built in 1856, was one of many grand hotels in Macon and was conveniently located at Fourth and Plum Streets across the street from the Union Railway passenger terminal. The Brown House burned twice, strangely on the same date 43 years apart, once in 1878 and again in 1921. This 1894 photograph shows the second Brown house, which was not rebuilt after the second fire. The WGXA-TV station occupies the site today.

PUBLIC BUILDINGS, HOTELS, AND ORGANIZATIONS

There were few places where African Americans could stay overnight in the 1900s until Charles Douglass founded the Douglass Hotel in 1908. Four years later, he established the Douglass Theatre, which became famous internationally as an African American vaudeville hall and a mecca for black entertainment. The Douglass Theatre launched the careers of Otis Redding, Little Richard, James Brown, and others. The theater closed in 1972 and the hotel several years before that, but the restored theater is again open for movies, performances, and special events.

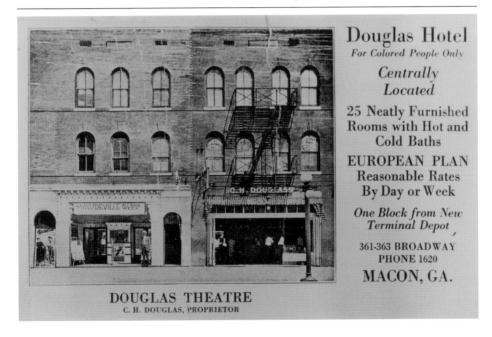

DOUGLAS THEATRE
C. H. DOUGLAS, PROPRIETOR

Douglas Hotel
For Colored People Only

Centrally Located

25 Neatly Furnished Rooms with Hot and Cold Baths

EUROPEAN PLAN
Reasonable Rates By Day or Week

One Block from New Terminal Depot

361-363 BROADWAY
PHONE 1620
MACON, GA.

The Dempsey Hotel, which featured a Japanese tearoom with costumed Japanese waitresses imported from New York, was built in 1912 at the corner of Cherry and Third Streets. Formerly the site of festive balls and candlelit dinners, the Dempsey began to decline in the 1960s. In 1983, it was redesigned into apartment units for the elderly and again enjoys full occupancy. (Courtesy the Georgia Archives Vanishing Georgia Collection BIBB-10.)

CHAPTER 3

A Sampling of Residences

The College Hill area contains grand homes of the antebellum and Victorian eras and is one of Macon's 11 historic districts. These beautiful residences are part of the 5,500 Macon and Bibb County structures listed on the National Register of Historic Places and have made Macon a favorite stop on Georgia's Antebellum Trail.

Woodruff House at 988 Bond Street is an 1836 Greek Revival home built by noted Macon architect Elam Alexander for railroad entrepreneur Jerry Cowles. In 1847, it became the home of the richest planter in Georgia, Joseph Bonds, who was murdered in 1859 by his former overseer after Bond dismissed him for mistreating one of Bond's 1,300 slaves. In 1887, it was the site of the 16th birthday ball of Winnie Davis, daughter of Jefferson Davis. Woodruff House is now owned by Mercer University and is used as a special event venue.

This elaborate Mediterranean villa located at 245 College Street was built for Nicholas Block around 1900 with no expense spared. Originally from Cincinnati, Block was a pioneer in the commercial manufacture of ice and president of Central City Ice Manufacturing. He also owned one of Macon's finest hotels of the time, the Dempsey. Samuel Coleman, the founder of Cherokee Brick Company, bought the house in 1923 and owned it until his death in 1949. It remains a private residence.

The Stevens-Gladstone House, located at 277 College Street, is an Italian Renaissance home of terra-cotta stucco. It was built around 1878 for Lewis O. Stevens, a Macon jeweler, and has an interesting mobile past. Originally located east of its present location, the home's owners purchased the house next-door, demolished it, and moved their home to the lot when Walnut Street was extended past College Street in the 1950s. It is now a bed-and-breakfast called the Venetian Mansion Inn.

A SAMPLING OF RESIDENCES

This Georgian residence (the Beall-Jordan-Dunlap House) at 315 College Street was built in 1860 for Nathan Beall, who amassed a fortune as a cotton plantation owner. Beall later sold it to Leonadius H. Jordan, a wealthy planter and proprietor of the Academy of Music. Jordan died in 1899, and his wife occupied the house until 1906. In 1969, the home was featured on the Allman Brothers' debut album, and in the 1970s and 1980s, it housed a popular restaurant, Beall's 1860 Inn. The Beall home was donated by its owners to Mercer University's School of Engineering in April 2009.

Built in 1886 by cotton merchant Calder Willingham, the Willingham-Hatcher House at 348 College Street was inherited in 1910 by his son, who conducted intensive renovations, drastically changing its appearance. The original cupola was removed, and the two smaller front and side porches were joined into one wraparound porch supported by columns of Georgia marble. The curved porch on the right, partially obscured by trees in the current photograph, echoes the lines of the original circular gazebo porch of the 1886 home. It is a private residence.

A SAMPLING OF RESIDENCES

The Walker-Shinholser-Rushin House at 397 College Street was built in 1889 as a redbrick Victorian but was redesigned in 1917 into its current Louis XVI French chateau style by Neel Reid. The famous Macon architect drew the plans for the exterior and personally supervised the interior decoration. It has been a boardinghouse, a therapeutic health spa, home for the Wesleyan College president for a time beginning in 1927, and is once again a private residence.

Built in 1875 by T. U. Conner, superintendent of the Academy for the Blind, the Stone-Boone-Flournoy House at 575 College Street exhibits Victorian influence. It was built of bricks that had been soaked in barrels of water so they wouldn't leach moisture from the mortar and had a metal roof imported from England. Except for the removal of the front porch and redesign of the front steps, the home retains much of its original look, the mortar still holds, and the house is still topped by a metal roof. It is a private residence.

A SAMPLING OF RESIDENCES

The Beaux-Arts-style McCaw-Massee House at 615 College Street is called the house that Crisco built. It was constructed in 1901 by Wallace McCaw, who invented a process for hydrogenating cottonseed oil that he manufactured in Macon under the name "Plantene." His formula was purchased by Proctor and Gamble, who changed the name of the product to Crisco. The company made McCaw one of its vice presidents and relocated him to Cincinnati, Ohio. The home was purchased in 1910 by W. Jordan Massee, a large man with a large personality who was a friend of Tennessee Williams. Massee was the inspiration for the character Big Daddy in Tennessee Williams's *Cat on a Hot Tin Roof*, which was written in the Massee house. In 1935, the house was converted into 13 apartments, but in 2002, it was restored to a single-family residence. (Courtesy of Dan Morton.)

The Pliny-Hall-Bennett House at 990 Georgia Avenue, a five-story Greek Revival townhouse, is sometimes referred to as "Uncle Pliny's house" after a former resident who is said to inhabit it in spite of having passed away. Built around 1902 on top of the spring and reservoir originally belonging to the Hay House, its basement contains a domed, circular chamber with a pool of water emanating from an underground spring, one of two water sources for the original inhabitants of Macon. The Bennett house is a private residence.

A Sampling of Residences

Located at 934 Georgia Avenue and completed in 1859, the Hay House (also known as the "Palace of the South"), a monumental Italian Renaissance Revival mansion built by William Johnston, encompasses more than 18,000 square feet in 24 rooms on 7 levels. It contains a secret room which legend says was used to hide the Confederate treasury, as Johnston was the comptroller for the Confederacy, but could have been used to hide guns, slaves, or the family's linens. The home remained in the family until 1926, when it was purchased by Parks Hay, whose heirs donated it to the Georgia Trust for Historic Preservation in 1977. The home is open to the public as one of Macon's three antebellum museums.

The Johnston house at 1021 Georgia Avenue was a Victorian mansion of redbrick built by Marshal Johnston in 1883. The president of the Confederacy, Jefferson Davis, and his family were guests of the Johnstons in 1887 for a reunion of Confederate veterans where Jefferson Davis addressed a parade of 45,000 from the balcony of the Johnston home. The structure was torn down in 1953 and replaced with a replica of Philadelphia's Independence Hall, built by an insurance company for its headquarters. The building now contains Mercer University's School of Law.

A SAMPLING OF RESIDENCES

The Nisbet House at 1032 Georgia Avenue was built around 1850 in the Old South architecture style for Eugenus Nisbet, known for penning Georgia's Ordinance of Secession in 1861. The residence was razed in 1972 along with the Roughton House, the Hanson House, and the Victorian Cottage on Nisbet Place by Southern Bell, who built a telephone exchange building of Southern-style architecture on the site. The original columns of the Nisbet house were preserved and used on the portico of the telephone building.

Built in 1840 for Judge Thaddeus Holt by renowned Macon builder Elam Alexander, the Holt House at 1129 Georgia Avenue is an outstanding example of Greek Revival architecture. A way of life long past is represented in its basement accommodations for servants and its wine and meat cellars. Judge Holt's granddaughter, Nanaline, was born in this house and married James Duke of North Carolina. The couple's daughter, Doris, nationally known as the "poor little rich girl," inherited the Duke tobacco fortune at the age of 12. Once the Carriage Stop Inn, it is again a private residence.

A SAMPLING OF RESIDENCES

Built about 1846 for Caldwell Raines, president of the Central Georgia Bank, the Raines-Miller-Carmichael House at 1183 Georgia Avenue is constructed in the shape of a Maltese cross, allowing every room exposure on three sides, with a porch connecting each arm of the cross. The front entrance porch originally followed the angles of the walls, but in the late 1800s, it was changed to its present circular shape. A highlight of the home is a three-story free-hanging circular staircase that goes from the foyer to the large dome-shaped cupola. It remains a private residence.

Sidney Lanier, famed Georgia poet, musician, and soldier, was born in this modest cottage at 935 High Street in 1842. The home, purchased in 1840 by Larkin Griffin, president of the Monroe Railroad and Banking Company, was rented at the time by Lanier's grandparents, and Lanier was born during a visit by his parents. The antebellum cottage is now open to the public. It houses the Sidney Lanier Museum and is owned by the Historic Macon Foundation.

A SAMPLING OF RESIDENCES

The Civil War came close to Macon when a cannonball fired by troops under the command of Gen. George Stoneman from across the Ocmulgee River bounced off a porch column of the 1853 home of Judge Asa Holt, crashed through the front of the house, and landed in the foyer. The unexploded cannonball was probably intended for the Hay House a block away, as Unionists believed the Confederate treasury was hidden there. It has been removed for safekeeping, but its indention in the wood floor can still be seen. Known as the Cannonball House and located at 356 Mulberry Street, it is open to the public as the third of Macon's antebellum home museums.

The brownstone town house at 566 Mulberry Street, designed by the New York architect who designed the Hay House and built by Italian artisans imported for that job, was constructed in 1858 for Dr. George Emerson. The ground floor, originally Dr. Emerson's office, was for many years occupied by the Palace Barber Shop, seen in this 1936 photograph. The top two floors, Dr. Emerson's residence, were later occupied for 80 years by Dr. W. B. Holmes, a dentist who had his office on the second floor and manufactured Holmes Mouthwash on the third floor.

This Neoclassic Revival residence at 635 Orange Street was built in 1900 by Dr. Albert B. Hinkle. In 1892, Dr. Hinkle and his father, Dr. J. B. Hinkle, were tried for the murder of Dr. J. J. Worsham, a dentist, at their office over a $65 dentist bill. J. B. Hinkle committed suicide by poison, and Albert was acquitted of Worsham's death. The Hinkle home has been converted into apartments.

The Munroe house at 159 Rogers Avenue was built in 1841 by Nathan Munroe, founder of the Georgia Academy for the Blind, facing Vineville Avenue, now several blocks away. Its appearance was greatly altered when ownership shifted to Charles Rogers in 1869. Rogers wanted the house to face the side street named for him but was unable to turn the house due to its brick facade. The entrances were reworked, and the side entrance facing Rogers Avenue became the front. It is a private residence.

A SAMPLING OF RESIDENCES

Villa Albicini at 150 Tucker Road was built by Daniel Hogan, a local florist, in the 1920s. Designed by famed Macon architect Neel Reid, Villa Albicini was named for 17th-century embroideries made under the supervision of Italian princess Albicini that still hang in the house. The villa was built on a piece of property cut from the Idle Hour Stock Farm, famous for the superior racehorses bred there and for its nationally acclaimed racetrack. Hogan began a nursery business, which he named the Idle Hour Nursery, on the property. It is a private residence.

The Baber House at 577 Walnut Street was built in 1831 as a residence for Dr. Ambrose Baber, Macon's first practicing physician, who died accidentally in 1846 after taking a dose of medicine he had prescribed for a patient. A pharmacist advised the patient that the dosage appeared too strong and, when questioned, the doctor confidently swallowed the prescription and died almost immediately. His residence was converted into a medical clinic in 1919 and a hospital, the Riverside, was added to the back in 1921. The building is the oldest remaining residence in the business district and is occupied by law offices.

A Sampling of Residences

CHAPTER 4

Work, Play, Schools, and Churches

Rutland School was built in 1910 as the state's first consolidated school. Previously, students walked to local schools, but consolidation necessitated transportation for them. This 1917 photograph shows the first school buses—horse- and mule-drawn wagons. By 1919, mules had been replaced by motor buses. (Courtesy of the Georgia Archives Vanishing Georgia Collection BIB-20.)

71

In 1826, Dr. Ambrose Baber led a movement to reserve acreage along the Ocmulgee River to build a city park for the health of the community. Formally established in 1828, Central City Park contained a mile-long horse-racing track said to be the finest and handsomest in the country, a bandstand, buildings for exhibitions, and an art gallery. The elaborate wooden entrance structure shown in the 1871 photograph below burned to the ground in 1913, at which time it was replaced by the current brick structures.

WORK, PLAY, SCHOOLS, AND CHURCHES

The site of concerts and gatherings since it was erected in 1871, this bandstand is one of few left in the country and is listed on the National Register of Historic Places. It was here that Jefferson Davis, on his last visit to Macon in 1887, held a special reception for children. The buildings surrounding the bandstand, built to display exhibitions for the state fair of that year, are now gone, and the bandstand is the only structure in this 1871 photograph that still exists.

This 1856 building at 86 Mulberry Street contained Charles Ells's thriving business, the Ells and Laney Store and Restaurant. The downstairs store sold general groceries and hardware. Above the store, the Ells family operated an oyster and refreshment saloon and a catering business. An advertisement in the Macon City Directory of 1860 stated, "All the delicacies of the seasons will be found on hand . . . all served by conscientious and courteous waiters," three of whom can be seen standing on the balcony.

Robert Plant, owner of the Idle Hour Stock Farm, was president of the First National Bank on the corner of Cherry and Second Streets, shown in 1866, and another small private bank. When these banks failed in 1904, Plant, who carried a $1-million life insurance policy on himself at premiums of $43,000 per year, committed suicide. The indication was that he deliberately sacrificed his life so that the customers of the bank should not suffer. SunTrust Bank is at the location today.

The officers and employees of Modern Flour Mills, manufacturer of Birdsey's Flour, are seen between 1910 and 1920 posing outside the company's main building on lower Poplar Street. The mills were purchased several years ago by ConAgra Foods and are still in use.

WORK, PLAY, SCHOOLS, AND CHURCHES

F. M. Haygood's store at 347 Cotton Avenue was the Macon agent for Howe's sewing machines and sold books, music, and other dry goods. Signs outside indicate the diversity of early commercial establishments. An ox-drawn wagon in this 1876 photograph taken by A. J. Haygood delivers merchandise in crates, barrels, and trunks. The building is now home to a Chinese restaurant. (Courtesy Georgia Archives Vanishing Georgia Collection BIB-82.)

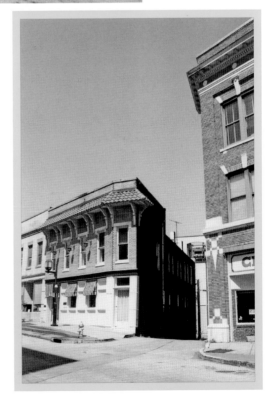

Schofield Iron Works, which produced cotton presses, cane mills, steam engines, boilers, and general machinery, was founded on Fifth Street by J. S. Schofield in 1850. By 1866, it was one of Macon's leading industries. During the Civil War, Schofield's and its fellow foundry, Findley's, melted down church and school bells to produce shot and shell for guns and cannons for Macon's defense. Schofield's eventually became Taylor Iron, which operated until the 1970s.

WORK, PLAY, SCHOOLS, AND CHURCHES

In the 1890 photograph below are two of Macon's 19th-century firehouses, Protection Engine No. 1 on the left and the Hook and Ladder Company at the center, in the middle of Poplar Street south of Second Street. The firehouses were conveniently located near cisterns placed in the exact center of intersections for convenience in filling the fire engines with water. Parks where the firehouses were once located now have water features symbolic of the old cisterns.

This building was constructed in 1916 at the corner of Broadway and Pine Streets for Happ Brothers Manufacturing, the city's largest downtown employer, which produced men's clothing for 60 years. During World War II, 80 percent of their production was used for military purposes, and a jacket designed by Happ was adopted for use by the U.S. Army. In 1999, the building was facing demolition with plans to sell the vintage bricks, considered to have more value than the building. The building was saved and has been converted to loft apartments.

WORK, PLAY, SCHOOLS, AND CHURCHES

In 1833, the Mercer Institute was founded in Penland, Georgia, by the Georgia Baptist Convention, and it was moved to Macon in 1870. It started as a school for young men preparing to enter the ministry and became Mercer University in 1839 when a female seminary was added. Initially, the entire college was housed in what is the now the administration building, seen in this 1894 photograph. Mercer, now a private coed university, offers programs in 11 diversified fields of study.

Chartered in 1836 under the guardianship and patronage of the Methodist Episcopal Church, Wesleyan College was the first institution of higher learning in the world to issue diplomas to female students. Called the Georgia Female College when it opened, the original structure, shown above, was designed and built by noted Macon architect Elam Alexander. The Federal Building containing the main Macon post office, located on the site today, was constructed to replicate the original Wesleyan building in appearance.

WORK, PLAY, SCHOOLS, AND CHURCHES

As Wesleyan grew, the campus expanded and the original building was incorporated into beautiful Victorian structures which were built around it. In 1928 the School of Liberal Arts was moved to Wesleyan's current location on Forsyth Road. Other departments followed and by the end of the 1950's the beautiful Victorian campus sat empty and dilapidated. In the early 1960's a fire furious enough to melt nearby cars raged through the campus, devouring it. The present Federal building containing the main Macon Post Office was built on the site in 1963.

Mount de Sales Academy, established in 1876 as a Catholic boarding academy for young ladies, first operated in the Colonial residence built for George Towns, governor of Georgia at 851 Orange Street. This 1901 photograph shows students of Mount de Sales playing lawn tennis in front of the original building. In 1910, it was demolished, and the academy buildings in their current form were built on the site. Mount de Sales is now a coed day institution for grades 6 through 12.

Elam Alexander was a noted Macon architect who built many distinguished homes and buildings, including Woodruff House and the original Wesleyan College buildings. Concerned about the education of poor children, when he died in 1863, he left funds to build Macon's first free public schools. Alexander Free School I, seen in this 1908 photograph, was built in 1883 at the corner of Pine and Second Streets from interest on bonds purchased for this purpose. It was the first of four schools to be constructed from Alexander's grant and was demolished in 1950, when a Kroger grocery store was built on the site. Wilson Electric, located next to the site, expanded into the Kroger building in the 1960s.

The original building of the Georgia Academy for the Blind, established in 1852 by Nathan Monroe, who realized the need for such a facility due to the temporary blindness of his young daughter, is seen in the 1852 photograph above. During the Civil War, the school was temporarily moved to Fort Valley, Georgia, and the building was used as a military hospital. Originally located at Orange and Forsyth Streets, the academy relocated in 1905 to Vineville Avenue, where it is located today. The city's first apartments, the Navarro, seen below, are on the original site.

WORK, PLAY, SCHOOLS, AND CHURCHES

Founded in 1868 through a strong friendship between William Appleton of New York, who was especially concerned about destitute orphans of Confederate soldiers, and Macon Episcopalian bishop John Beckwith, Appleton's Children's Home cared for children from infancy through age 18. The residents were moved from 753 College Street to a new location in 1924, and the original Appleton's building became St. Paul's Episcopal Church's parish house.

Christ Episcopal Church was founded in 1825 and was the first congregation organized in Macon. This Gothic building, shown in a 1925 photograph, was the church's second and was built in 1851 utilizing material from the first church building, which was taken down in 1850. The church's bell, used in both the first and current buildings, was donated in 1863 as a patriotic offering to the Confederacy to be melted down to make cannons to protect Macon. The current bell, bearing the inscription "On earth, peace, goodwill to men" was contributed by church member A. A. Roff in 1864.

WORK, PLAY, SCHOOLS, AND CHURCHES

Mulberry Street United Methodist Church, built in 1828 as a small wooden structure, was the first church building of any denomination erected in Macon. The small sanctuary was replaced with a fine brick edifice, which later burned. The current sanctuary is the fourth, but all four have been located at the original site, which has never been anything but a church. Mulberry United Methodist Church is known as "The Old Mother" of Methodism in Georgia and has always been closely associated with Wesleyan College, a Methodist institution.

St. Joseph's Catholic Church, a Romanesque neo-Gothic church, took 14 years to build at a cost of $1 million in the late 1880s. It was dedicated in 1903 and is considered one of the most elegant church buildings in the South. The interior contains 57 Bavarian stained glass windows and marble carvings, statues, and altars from the Carrera quarries in Italy. The residences to the right of the church in the old photograph have been replaced by the church's parish house.

WORK, PLAY, SCHOOLS, AND CHURCHES

The First Baptist Church of Christ was established in 1826. After fires destroyed earlier structures, the high Victorian Gothic style sanctuary of today was dedicated in 1887. The interior of the sanctuary is built like the inverted hull of a ship, a unique Gothic feature. The streetcar in the 1890s photograph below is electrified, but earlier streetcars were pulled by mules. The deacons of the church were said to chastise the mule drivers because the colorful language they directed at the mules drifted into the church's open windows.

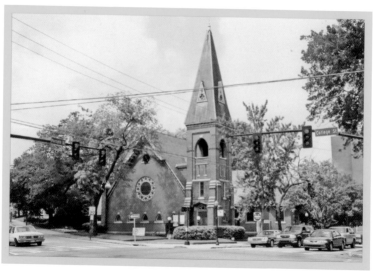

St. Paul's Episcopal Church was originally on the site of one of Macon's earliest railroad yards, that of the Monroe Railroad. The tracks were laid in 1838, and a freight warehouse was built to handle shipments of cotton. In 1869, the warehouse, which was at the site of the current St. Paul's Apartments, was modified into a church, seen in this 1873 photograph, and a beautiful round stained glass window was added. In 1884, the present Romanesque Gothic church was erected utilizing brick and the stained glass window from the pervious structure.

WORK, PLAY, SCHOOLS, AND CHURCHES

The First Church of Christ Scientist met in the Macon public library building on Mulberry Street before building its current location at the corner of Georgia Avenue and Arlington Place. This 1920 photograph shows children playing in piles of dirt in front of the Georgia Avenue building, still in use today, while it was under construction.

First Presbyterian Church was built
in 1856 at Mulberry and First Streets
in a combination of Romanesque and
12th-century Norman architectural
design. At the time it was built, its
steeple was the tallest in the state.
Macon's first town clock was donated
to the church when a new clock was
installed in the courthouse tower. It was
incorporated into the steeple but was
later removed because its gonging was
out of sync with that of the courthouse
clock across the street. The clock is
visible in the historical photograph at
right but missing from the modern
photograph below.

In 1890, the pastor of Tattnall Square Presbyterian traveled to lumberyards in Macon and surrounding cities to secure lumber to build a permanent house of worship for his congregation, often paying for it by preaching. The building at 1096 College Street, which his efforts produced, was dedicated in May 1891. Originally called Second Presbyterian, the name Tattnall Square Presbyterian Church was first used in 1893.

Discover Thousands of Local History Books Featuring Millions of Vintage Images

Arcadia Publishing, the leading local history publisher in the United States, is committed to making history accessible and meaningful through publishing books that celebrate and preserve the heritage of America's people and places.

Find more books like this at
www.arcadiapublishing.com

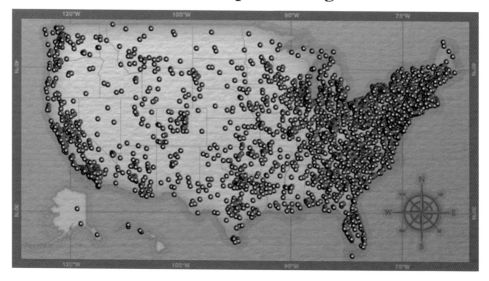

Search for your hometown history, your old stomping grounds, and even your favorite sports team.